MOTHER AND SON
BACK AND FORTH JOURNAL

Mom and Me
Copyright © 2021 by Skribent

First paperback edition April 2021

A mother-son relationship...what a wonderful and emotionally overwhelming bond!

A healthy relationship between mother and son is of utmost importance. A positive and strong bond has an immense influence on a boy's personality. Furthermore, a boy who is loved and cared for by his mother grows up to be a confident and happy man.

Open and honest communication, from early childhood, between mother and son, is the basis of a lasting and good relationship.

Growing up can truly be a stressful experience. Moreover, we know sometimes boys communicate a lot through actions rather than with words. They might need some encouragement and help from their parents to talk about their experiences and emotions. A journal like this gives both of you, mom and son, the opportunity to express your true feelings, get to know each other more every day, and create a loving and strong relationship.

For an everlasting connection!

Pieces of Advice:

Throughout the book, there are pages, with the title " Mom" or "Son". If the word "Son" is at the top, the boy should reply or write on that page. If the word "Mom" is at the top, mom must be the one to reply and write on that page.
Pages with the title "We can do this together"...are for both of you to reply, write or draw.

Before beginning, set a schedule to reply to all the questions. Decide:
- Who is allowed to see the book
- How will you pass the journal back and forth
- When can you expect a response

But remember...

Write your own rules,
be completely honest
and
have so much fun.

MOM

BASIC INFORMATION....

My Name:

_____

_____

Where and when I was born:

_____

_____

Nicknames:

_____

_____

Hair Color (when I was born):

_____

Hair Color (at the moment):

_____

Height:

_____

SON

WHAT ABOUT ME?

My Name:

_____

_____

Where and when I was born:

_____

_____

Nicknames:

_____

_____

Hair Color (when I was born):

_____

Hair Color (right now):

_____

Height:

_____

MOM

My favorite animal:

_____

My favorite color:

_____

My favorite food:

_____

My favorite drink:

_____

My favorite fruit:

_____

My favorite word:

_____

How would I describe myself in one word:

_____

SON

My favorite animal:

_____

My favorite color:

_____

My favorite food:

_____

My favorite drink:

_____

My favorite fruit:

_____

My favorite word:

_____

How would I describe myself in one word:

_____

MOM

THIS IS A DRAWING OF MY WONDERFUL SON

SON

MOM, LET ME DRAW A PICTURE OF YOU

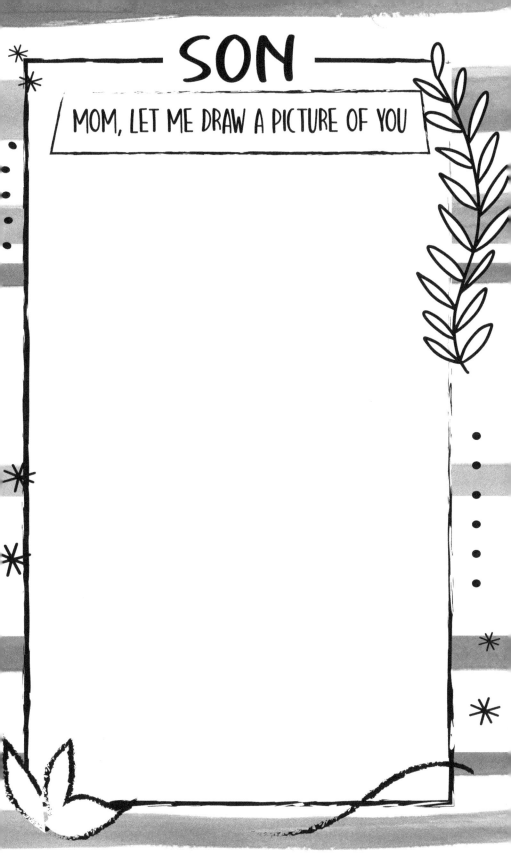

MOM

My favorite scent is:

_____

My favorite book and why:

_____

_____

_____

_____

It makes me happy:

_____

_____

A home is...

_____

_____

_____

SON

My favorite scent is:

_____

My favorite book and why:

_____

_____

_____

_____

It makes me happy:

_____

_____

A home is...

_____

_____

_____

MOM

One word to describe my childhood:

_____

My most cherished childhood memories:

_____

_____

_____

My best friend was:

_____

This is the best prank I played on my friends:

_____

_____

_____

_____

SON

One word to describe my childhood:

_____

My most wonderful memory so far:

_____

_____

My best friend is:

_____

The most incredible adventure I had
with my best friend :

_____

_____

_____

_____

Mom, tell me...

What was your relationship with your parents like? Were they strict?

_____

_____

What rule was the hardest to follow when you were a child?

_____

_____

How was school like for you?

_____

_____

What is the craziest thing you've ever done?

_____

_____

_____

Son, tell me...

Something you love about our family:

_____

_____

What is one rule you would change at home? Why?

_____

_____

How do you truly feel at school?

_____

_____

Describe a perfect school day:

_____

_____

_____

_____

MOM

Things my mom told me as a kid:

_____

_____

_____

_____

_____

An advice I would give to my younger self:

_____

_____

_____

_____

SON

Things you always say to me:

_____
_____
_____
_____
_____
_____

An advice I would give to my old self:

_____
_____
_____
_____
_____
_____

MOM

DRAWING OF OUR FAMILY AS SUPERHEROS

SON

DRAWING OF OUR FAMILY AS SUPERHEROS

MOM

Something I did as a kid that annoyed my parents:

_____

_____

_____

_____

A beautiful memory about my grandparents:

_____

_____

_____

_____

_____

SON

One of the most funniest moments I've shared with you, mom:

_____

_____

_____

_____

What I will always remember about my granparents:

_____

_____

_____

_____

_____

_____

MOM

Son, when I was a kid I wanted to be:

_____

Let me tell you why:

_____

_____

_____

_____

I am thankful for:

_____

_____

_____

_____

_____

SON

Mom, when I grow up I want to be:

_____

Let me tell you why:

_____

_____

_____

_____

I am thankful for:

_____

_____

_____

_____

_____

MOM

MY PERFECT DAY

_____

_____

_____

_____

_____

_____

_____

...AND A DRAWING OF MY PERFECT DAY

SON

MY PERFECT DAY

_____

_____

_____

_____

_____

_____

_____

...AND A DRAWING OF MY PERFECT DAY

MOM

My favorite movie:

_____

My favorite tv show:

_____

My favorite sport:

_____

I am afraid of:

_____

My favorite book:

_____

My favorite literary character:

_____

My favorite video game:

_____

SON

My favorite movie:

_____

My favorite tv show:

_____

My favorite sport:

_____

I am afraid of:

_____

My favorite book:

_____

My favorite storybook character:

_____

My favorite video game:

_____

Mom, tell me...

What were you like in high school?

_____

_____

What was the hardest thing about high school?

_____

_____

What sports you played in high school?

_____

_____

What is your favorite memory from high school?

_____

_____

_____

Son, tell me...

What are your favorite subjects at school? Why?

_____

_____

What are your favorite activities at school?

_____

_____

Three things you hate about school:

_____

_____

_____

_____

_____

_____

MOM

My superhero name and superpowers:

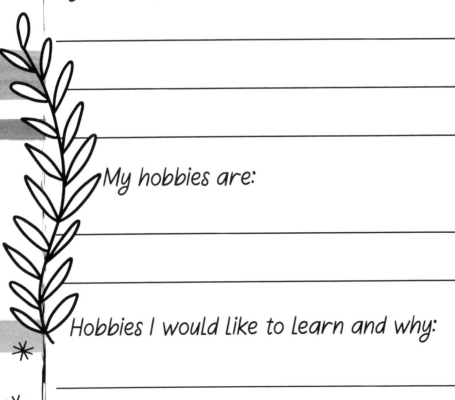

_____

_____

_____

My hobbies are:

_____

_____

Hobbies I would like to learn and why:

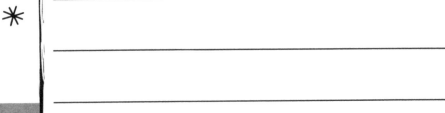

_____

_____

_____

_____

_____

SON

My superhero name and superpowers:

_____

_____

_____

My hobbies are:

_____

_____

Hobbies I would like to learn and why:

_____

_____

_____

_____

_____

MOM

DRAWING:
YOUR FAVORITE GAME OR VIDEO GAME

SON

DRAWING:
YOUR FAVORITE HOBBY

Mom, tell me...

How did you meet Dad?

_____

_____

_____

_____

_____

One of the most romantic things you did
with Dad:

_____

_____

_____

_____

Son, tell me...

What do you admire in other boys your age? Why?

_____

_____

_____

_____

Something you are really looking forward. Why?

_____

_____

_____

_____

_____

Mom, tell me...

When did you realize you wanted to have kids? How many kids did you want?

_____

_____

_____

What was the day I was born like?

_____

Were you nervous? Why?

_____

_____

_____

What did I look like as a baby?

_____

_____

Son, tell me...

How would you cheer up a friend?

_____

_____

_____

What rules would you change at school?

_____

_____

_____

If you could quit school and do anything you wanted all day, what would it be?

_____

_____

_____

Mom, tell me...

How did you choose my name?

_____

_____

What were my first words?

_____

_____

_____

What's the first toy you bought me?

_____

What is the funniest thing I did as a small kid?

_____

_____

_____

Son, tell me...

A good joke:

_____

_____

_____

_____

Now, tell me something gross:

_____

_____

One thing you could eat for the rest of your life:

_____

If you could create a new holiday, what it would be:

_____

_____

MOM

Why it's great to be an adult:

_____

_____

_____

If I could change my name, I would choose:

_____

A mountain I would love to climb:

_____

_____

Where I would go for a one month trip:

_____

_____

_____

SON

What I love about being a kid:

_____

_____

_____

If I could change my name, I would choose:

_____

A mountain I would love to climb:

_____

_____

Where I would go for a long, long trip:

_____

_____

_____

MOM

DRAWING:
SOME OF YOUR GOOFY FACES

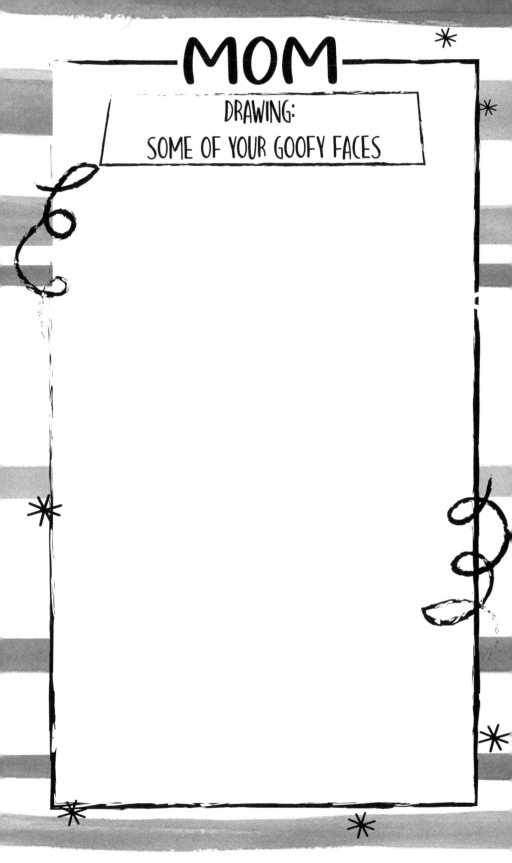

SON

DRAWING:
SOME OF YOUR GOOFY FACES

MOM

My last dream was about...

_____

_____

_____

_____

_____

What would I do with USD $100 million
dollars:

_____

_____

_____

_____

_____

_____

SON

My last dream was about...

_____

_____

_____

_____

_____

What would I do with USD $100 million dollars:

_____

_____

_____

_____

_____

_____

MOM

Grey, Blue or Yellow:

_____

Pizza, Burger or Hot dog:

_____

Train, Plane or Car:

_____

Hot chocolate, Tea or Orange juice:

_____

Football, Tennis or Baseball:

_____

Adventure, RPG or Puzzle :

_____

December, August or January:

_____

SON

Grey, Blue or Yellow:

_____

Pizza, Burger or Hot dog:

_____

Train, Plane or Car:

_____

Hot chocolate, Tea or Orange juice:

_____

Football, Tennis or Baseball:

_____

Adventure, RPG or Puzzle :

_____

December, August or January:

_____

MOM

15 THINGS I WOULD LIKE TO DO WITH YOU

SON

15 THINGS I WOULD LIKE TO DO WITH YOU

Mom, tell me...

What would you change of your life:

_____

_____

_____

_____

_____

If you could do something crazy right now, what would you do?

_____

_____

_____

_____

_____

_____

Son, tell me...

What would you change of your life:

_____

_____

_____

_____

_____

If you could do something crazy right now, what would you do?

_____

_____

_____

_____

_____

_____

SON,
YOU WILL
OUTGROW
MY LAP,
BUT
NEVER
MY HEART

MOM *

I WOULD LIKE TO INVENT THIS...

SON *

I WOULD LIKE TO INVENT THIS...

Mom, tell me...

IF YOU HAD TO GIVE EVERYBODY IN OUR FAMILY NEW NAMES, WHAT WOULD THEY BE?

Son, tell me... ✳

IF YOU HAD TO GIVE EVERYBODY IN OUR FAMILY NEW NAMES, WHAT WOULD THEY BE?

_____

_____

_____

_____

_____

_____

_____

_____

_____

_____

_____

_____

_____

MOM

MY HOPES AND DREAMS FOR YOU

_____

_____

_____

_____

_____

_____

_____

_____

_____

_____

_____

_____

_____

_____

_____

SON

MY HOPES AND DREAMS FOR YOU

_____

_____

_____

_____

_____

_____

_____

_____

_____

_____

_____

_____

_____

MOM

MY BEST TRIP EVER

_____

_____

_____

_____

_____

A DRAWING OF MY BEST TRIP EVER

* SON

MY BEST TRIP EVER

_____

_____

_____

_____

_____

A DRAWING OF MY BEST TRIP EVER

We can do this together

JUST THINK OF SOMETHING YOU BOTH WOULD LIKE TO DO AND DO IT, WITHOUT THINKING TOO MUCH. AFTERWARDS, DESCRIBE YOUR EXPERIENCE.

_____

_____

_____

_____

_____

_____

_____

_____

_____

_____

_____

_____

_____

We can do this *together

DRAWING OF OUR ADVENTURE

Mom, tell me... *

What makes you angry:

_____

_____

_____

What makes you sad:

_____

_____

_____

What makes you laugh:

_____

_____

_____

_____

Son, tell me... *

What makes you angry:

_____

_____

_____

What makes you sad:

_____

_____

_____

What makes you laugh:

_____

_____

_____

_____

Mom, tell me...

Is there a television show character that reminds you of me? Who and why?

_____

_____

_____

What is my worst habit?

_____

_____

What is your most embarassing moment?

_____

_____

_____

_____

_____

_____

Son, tell me...

Is there a cartoon character that reminds you of me? Who and why?

_____

_____

_____

What is my worst habit?

_____

_____

What is your most embarassing moment?

_____

_____

_____

_____

_____

MOM

Let me tell you the best and worst parts of being a mother

_____

_____

_____

_____

_____

_____

_____

_____

_____

_____

_____

_____

_____

SON

Let me tell you the best and worst parts of being your son

_____

_____

_____

_____

_____

_____

_____

_____

_____

_____

_____

_____

Mom, tell me...

The nicest and meanest thing I've ever said to you:

_____

_____

_____

_____

_____

How do you have fun with your friends?

_____

_____

_____

_____

_____

_____

Son, tell me...

The nicest and meanest thing I've ever said to you:

_____

_____

_____

_____

_____

How do you have fun with your friends?

_____

_____

_____

_____

_____

_____

MOM

Son, let me give you an advice:

_____
_____
_____
_____
_____
_____
_____
_____
_____
_____
_____
_____
_____
_____
_____
_____

SON

Mom, let me give you an advice:

_____

_____

_____

_____

_____

_____

_____

_____

_____

_____

_____

_____

MOM

If I could have three whishes, they would be:

_____

_____

_____

_____

_____

_____

_____

_____

_____

_____

_____

_____

_____

SON

If I could have three whishes, they would be:

_____

_____

_____

_____

_____

_____

_____

_____

_____

_____

_____

_____

_____

_____

We can do this together

PLAN A PERFECT PICNIC FOR BOTH OF YOU.
DESCRIBE THE DETAILS HERE.

_____
_____
_____
_____
_____
_____
_____
_____
_____
_____
_____
_____
_____
_____
_____

We can do this together

DRAWING OF YOUR PICNIC

MOM

Would you rather go fishing or hiking:

_____

Would you rather live in a treehouse or in an igloo:

_____

Would you rather have 6 fingers on each hand or 4 toes on each foot:

_____

Would you rather go into the future or into the past:

_____

Would you rather eat only pizza for a year or only ice cream for a month:

_____

SON

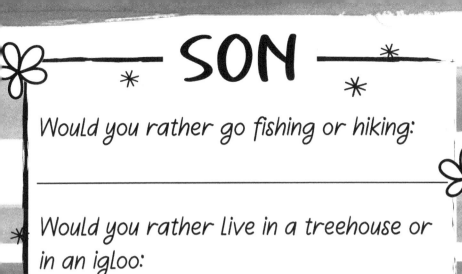

Would you rather go fishing or hiking:

_____

Would you rather live in a treehouse or
in an igloo:

_____

Would you rather have 6 fingers on
each hand or 4 toes on each foot:

_____

Would you rather go into the future or
into the past:

_____

Would you rather eat only pizza for a
year or only ice cream for a month:

_____

MOM

Son, your best talents are...

_____

_____

_____

_____

_____

Three things you can improve on...

_____

_____

_____

_____

_____

_____

SON

Mom, your best talents are...

_____

_____

_____

_____

_____

Three things you can improve on...

_____

_____

_____

_____

_____

_____

MOM

DRAWING:
YOU AND ME

SON

DRAWING:
YOU AND ME

A
MESSY BUN
IS THE CROWN
OF A
MOM

MOM

Son, I'm so very proud of you for:

_____

_____

_____

_____

_____

_____

_____

_____

_____

_____

_____

_____

_____

_____

SON

Mom, I'm so proud of you for:

_____

_____

_____

_____

_____

_____

_____

_____

_____

_____

_____

_____

_____

_____

_____

_____

Mom, tell me...

How do you see yourself 20 years from now:

_____

_____

_____

_____

_____

DRAW A PICTURE

Son, tell me...

How do you see yourself 20 years from now:

_____

_____

_____

_____

_____

DRAW A PICTURE

MOM

· · · · · · ·

Three happiest moments of my life so far:

_____

_____

_____

_____

_____

_____

One thing I would change about myself:

_____

_____

_____

_____

_____

_____

SON

· · · · · ·

Three happiest moments of my Life so far:

_____

_____

_____

_____

_____

_____

One thing I would change about myself:

_____

_____

_____

_____

_____

MOM

What would you do if a friend asks you to keep a secret?

_____

_____

_____

_____

_____

How would you change our world?

_____

_____

_____

_____

_____

_____

— SON —

What would you do if a friend asks you to keep a secret?

_____

_____

_____

_____

_____

How would you change our world?

_____

_____

_____

_____

_____

_____

MOM

Would you rather be wolverine or superman:

_____

Would you rather be an unknown superhero or a famous villain:

_____

Would you rather spend a weekend with ninjas or with artists:

_____

Would you rather be a cop or an astronaut:

_____

Would you rather have 3 wishes granted today or 10 wishes granted thirty years from now:

_____

SON

Would you rather be wolverine or superman:

_____

Would you rather be an unknown superhero or a famous villain:

_____

Would you rather spend a weekend with ninjas or with artists:

_____

Would you rather be a cop or an astronaut:

_____

Would you rather have 3 wishes granted today or 10 wishes granted thirty years from now:

_____

MOM

DRAWING:
HAPPINESS

SON

DRAWING: HAPPINESS

MOM

If I could bring an object to life, it would be:

_____

_____

_____

_____

_____

Five things I would grab if my house was on fire:

_____

_____

_____

_____

_____

SON

If I could bring an object to life, it would be:

_____

_____

_____

_____

Five things I would grab if my house was on fire:

_____

_____

_____

_____

_____

MOM

Favorite kind of music:

_____

The craziest thing I've ever eaten:

_____

The funniest word I know:

_____

A famous person I would like to meet:

_____

A chore I hate doing at home:

_____

What would I do if I was president for a day:

_____

_____

SON

Favorite kind of music:

_____

The craziest thing I've ever eaten:

_____

The funniest word I know:

_____

A famous person I would like to meet:

_____

A chore I hate doing at home:

_____

What would I do if I was president for a day:

_____

_____

_____

MOM

A name I would give to my baby dinosaur:

_____

My favorite weird food:

_____

If I could travel into space, I would go to...

_____

My favorite vegetable:

_____

The ugliest name I've ever heard:

_____

A popular song that annoys me a lot:

_____

If I were an animal I would be...

_____

SON

A name I would give to my baby dinosaur:

_____

My favorite weird food:

_____

If I could travel into space, I would go to...

_____

My favorite vegetable:

_____

The ugliest name I've ever heard:

_____

A popular song that annoys me a lot:

_____

If I were an animal I would be...

_____

MOM

Would you rather live 90 years in poverty on 40 years in riches:

_____

Would you rather play a video game or a board game:

_____

Would you rather team up with Captain America or with Wonder Woman:

_____

Would you rather be invisible or have supernatural strength:

_____

Would you rather walk with your hands for a year or eat with your feet for three months:

_____

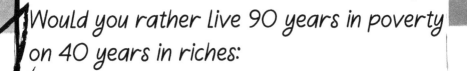

— SON —

Would you rather live 90 years in poverty on 40 years in riches:

_____

Would you rather play a video game or a board game:

_____

Would you rather team up with Captain America or with Wonder Woman:

_____

Would you rather be invisible or have supernatural strength:

_____

Would you rather walk with your hands for a year or eat with your feet for three months:

_____

— MOM —

DRAWING:
EVERYTHING THAT COMES TO MY MIND BUT
USING ONLY THREE COLORS

SON

DRAWING:
EVERYTHING THAT COMES TO MY MIND BUT USING ONLY THREE COLORS

Mom, tell me...

What is your favorite season?

_____

You have fun with our family when we...

_____

_____

_____

What is your favorite part of the day?

_____

Who is your favorite superhero?

_____

If you were invisible for a day what would you do:

_____

_____

_____

Son, tell me...

What is your favorite season?

_____

You have fun with our family when we...

_____

_____

_____

What is your favorite part of the day?

_____

Who is your favorite superhero?

_____

If you were invisible for a day what would you do:

_____

_____

_____

Mom, tell me...

✳ ✳ ✳ ✳ ✳

What worries you the most?

_____

_____

_____

_____

_____

_____

How fortunate do you think you are?

_____

_____

_____

_____

_____

_____

Son, tell me...

* * * * * *

What worries you the most?

_____

_____

_____

_____

_____

How fortunate do you think you are?

_____

_____

_____

_____

_____

Mom, tell me...

If you could change 5 things you did wrong in the past, what would they be?

_____

_____

_____

_____

_____

_____

_____

_____

_____

_____

_____

_____

_____

_____

Son, tell me...

If you could change 5 things you did wrong in the past, what would they be?

_____

_____

_____

_____

_____

_____

_____

_____

_____

_____

_____

_____

_____

MOM

A DRAWING OF OUR HOME

SON

A DRAWING OF OUR HOME

MOM

Son, let me tell you something that you probably don't know about me:

_____

_____

_____

_____

_____

_____

_____

_____

_____

_____

_____

_____

_____

_____

SON

Mom, let me tell you something that you probably don't know about me:

_____

_____

_____

_____

_____

_____

_____

_____

_____

_____

_____

_____

_____

MOM

Son, I love you because:

_____

_____

_____

_____

_____

_____

_____

_____

_____

_____

_____

_____

_____

_____

SON

Mom, I love you because:

_____
_____
_____
_____
_____
_____
_____
_____
_____
_____
_____
_____
_____
_____

MOM

I WOULD LIKE TO ASK YOU SOMETHING ELSE

SON

I WOULD LIKE TO ASK YOU SOMETHING ELSE

MOM

_____

_____

_____

_____

_____

_____

_____

_____

_____

_____

_____

_____

_____

_____

_____

_____

SON

MOM

SON

MOM

AN SPECIAL LETTER JUST FOR YOU

SON

AN SPECIAL LETTER JUST FOR YOU

MOM

SON

MOM

SON

We thank you for choosing us.
We would really appreciate if you leave us
an honest review.
Until next time!

9 781802 322576